Ms. Frizzle's Adventures
MEDIEVAL CASTLE

Ms. Frizzle's Adventures
MEDIEVAL CASTLE

A JOUSTING TOURNAMENT WAS A MEDIEVAL FESTIVAL WHERE KNIGHTS FROM ALL OVER COMPETED IN FIGHTING CONTESTS.

THIS BULLETIN BOARD MADE BY MS. FRIZZLE'S CLASS

Tents where Knights got dressed

For the joust, Knights wore special armor that was stronger and fancier.

Knights jousted with Wooden lances. Even though this was a game, Knights were sometimes hurt or killed.

Every Knight had his own colors.

The horse wore the Knight's colors, too.

Ms. Frizzle's Adventures
MEDIEVAL CASTLE

by **JOANNA COLE**
illustrated by **BRUCE DEGEN**

SCHOLASTIC INC.
New York Toronto London Auckland Sydney
Mexico City New Delhi Hong Kong Buenos Aires

ISBN 0-590-10821-2 • 10 9 8 7 6 5 4 3 2 1   04 05 06 07 08
Printed in the U.S.A. • 08 • First paperback edition, September 2004.
The text type was set in GillSans. • The illustrator used pen and ink, water-color, color pencil, and gouache for the paintings in this book. • The author thanks Carol Hart and her children, Jamieson, Rose, and Phoebe, for giving her the idea to write about castles. • The author and illustrator would like to thank Nancy Wu of The Cloisters Museum and The Metropolitan Museum of Art for her careful review of the manuscript and illustrations.

For Sir Cooper Garff
—J.C.

For Janet Carlile,
whose friendship and love
have withstood the siege of time
in the Castle Keep of our hearts
—B.D.

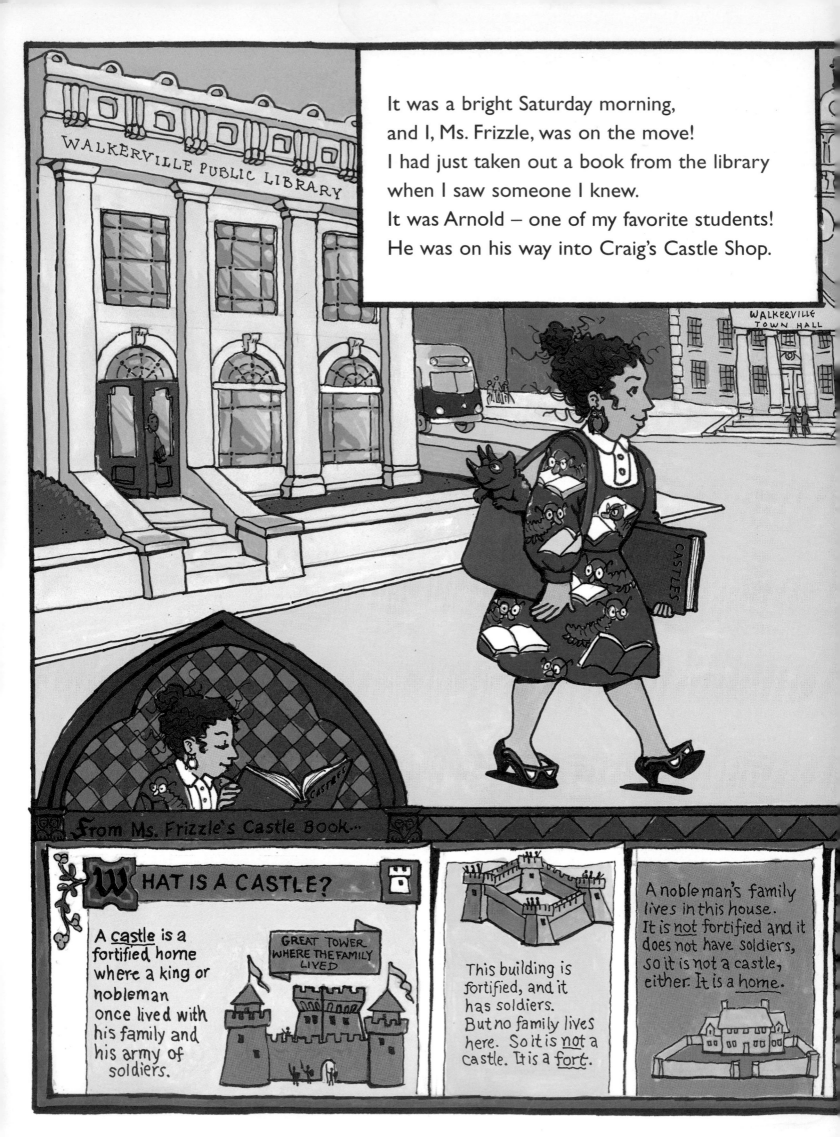

WALKERVILLE PUBLIC LIBRARY

WALKERVILLE TOWN HALL

It was a bright Saturday morning,
and I, Ms. Frizzle, was on the move!
I had just taken out a book from the library
when I saw someone I knew.
It was Arnold – one of my favorite students!
He was on his way into Craig's Castle Shop.

From Ms. Frizzle's Castle Book...

WHAT IS A CASTLE?

A **castle** is a fortified home where a king or nobleman once lived with his family and his army of soldiers.

GREAT TOWER WHERE THE FAMILY LIVED

This building is fortified, and it has soldiers. But no family lives here. So it is <u>not</u> a castle. It is a <u>fort</u>.

A nobleman's family lives in this house. It is <u>not</u> fortified and it does not have soldiers, so it is not a castle, either. It is a <u>home</u>.

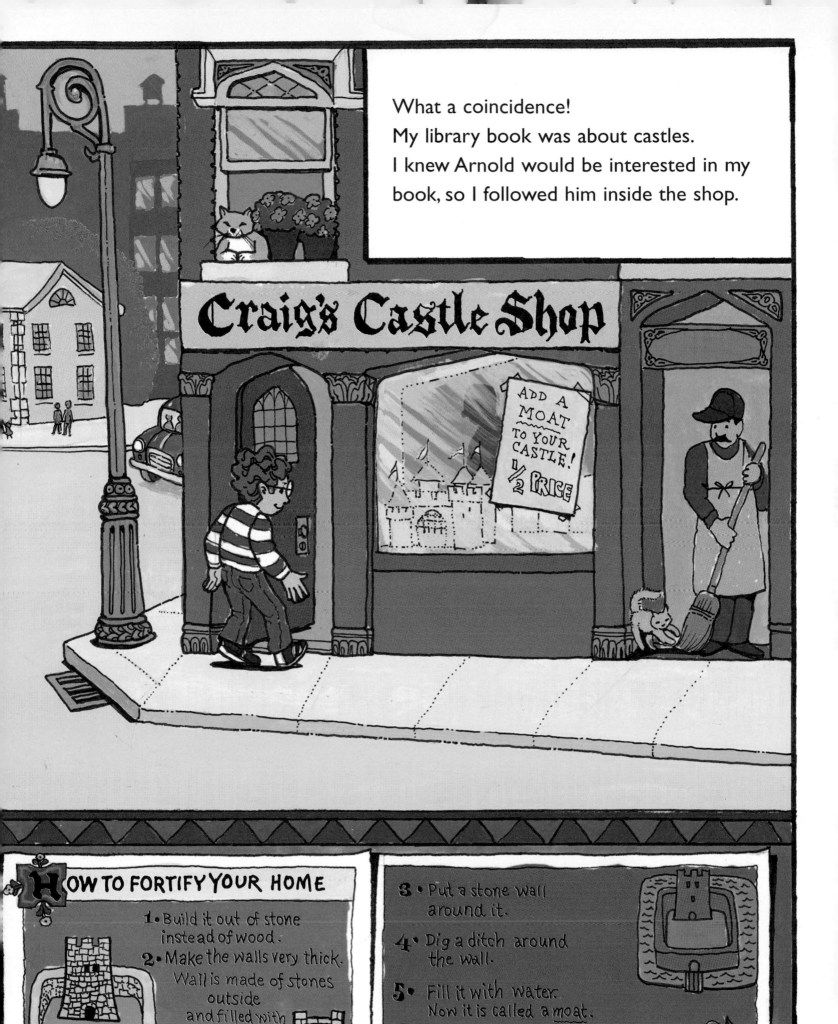

What a coincidence!
My library book was about castles.
I knew Arnold would be interested in my book, so I followed him inside the shop.

Craig's Castle Shop

ADD A MOAT TO YOUR CASTLE! 1/2 PRICE

HOW TO FORTIFY YOUR HOME

1. Build it out of stone instead of wood.
2. Make the walls very thick. Wall is made of stones outside and filled with rubble inside.
3. Put a stone wall around it.
4. Dig a ditch around the wall.
5. Fill it with water. Now it is called a moat.
6. Make openings for soldiers to shoot from.

WHERE WERE CASTLES?
There were castles
all around the world,
but Europe and England,
Scotland, Ireland, and Wales
had the most castles.

AFRICAN CASTLE

MIDDLE EASTERN CASTLE

SPANISH CASTLE

JAPANESE CASTLE

CRAIG, MEET MS. FRIZZLE.

NOT MY TEACHER!
IT'S SATURDAY!

HELLO, MS. DRESS...OOPS!
I MEAN, MS. FRIZZLE.

Everywhere in the shop there were
models of castles from all over the world.
And there were shelves and shelves of figurines.
Craig, the shop owner, was showing Arnold
a collection of people for an English castle.
Arnold and Craig both gave me a warm welcome!

ENGLISH CASTLE

I couldn't help noticing
a handle on the floor.
Since I, Ms. Frizzle,
am naturally curious,
I experimented by pulling on it.
It was a trapdoor to the basement.
Arnold is always so adventurous!
He insisted on going down.
Naturally, I followed him,
and Craig came down to join us.

When Arnold found a mysterious tunnel lit by flaming torches, I went along. Craig and Crystal did, too.

Arnold wanted to see where the passage
went, so he ran faster and faster.
I, Ms. Frizzle, kept up the pace,
and Craig and Crystal followed us eagerly.
Finally, we saw light at the end of
the tunnel.

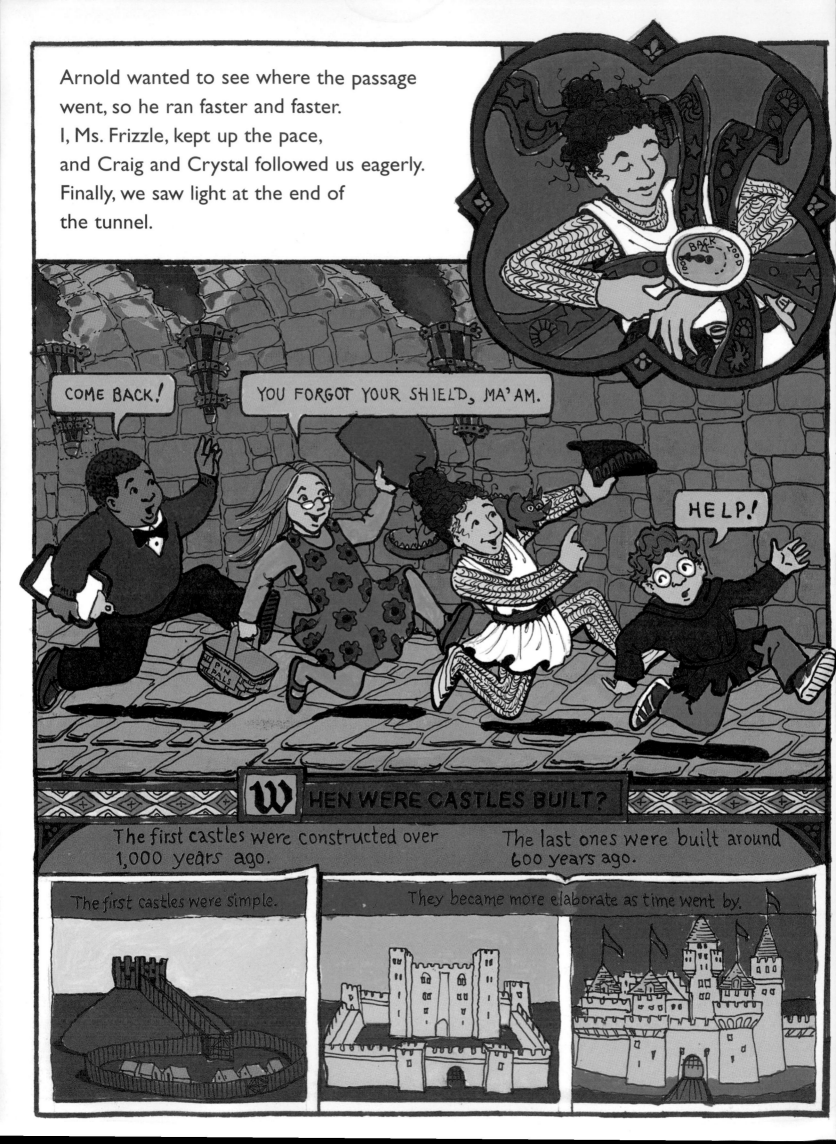

COME BACK!

YOU FORGOT YOUR SHIELD, MA'AM.

HELP!

W HEN WERE CASTLES BUILT?

The first castles were constructed over
1,000 years ago.

The last ones were built around
600 years ago.

The first castles were simple.

They became more elaborate as time went by.

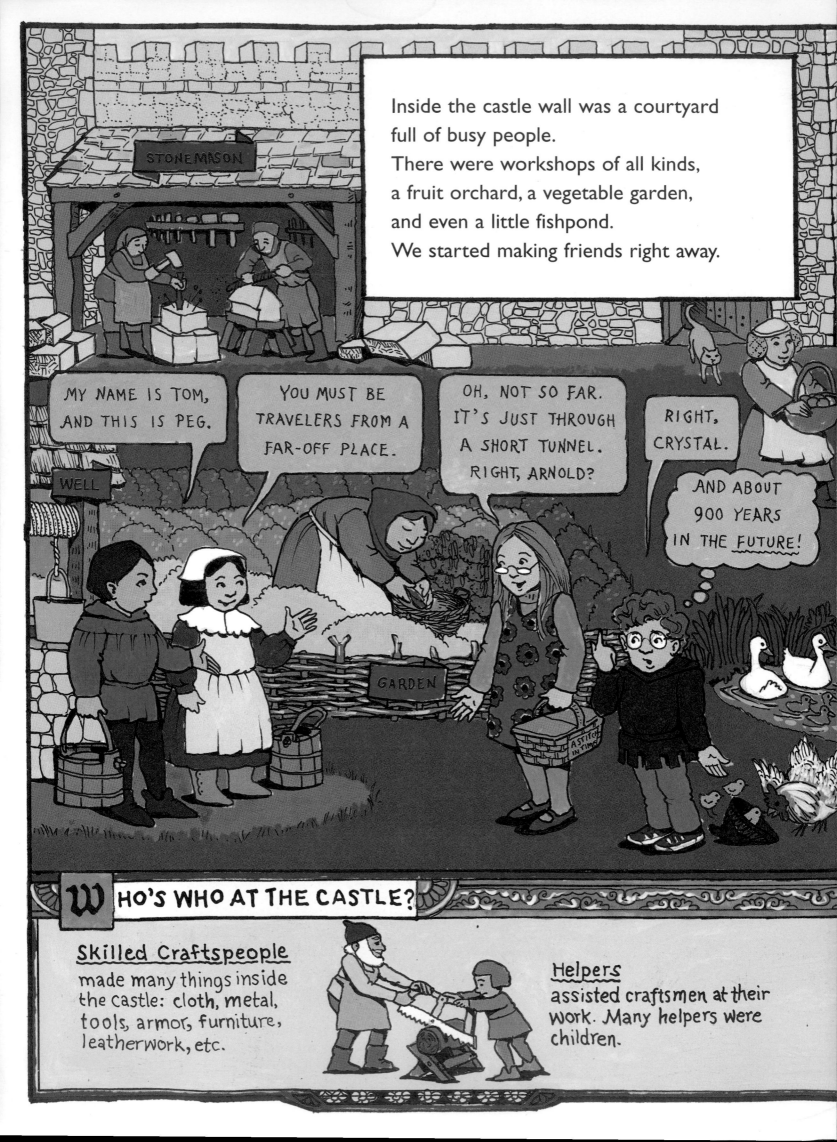

Inside the castle wall was a courtyard full of busy people.
There were workshops of all kinds, a fruit orchard, a vegetable garden, and even a little fishpond.
We started making friends right away.

WHO'S WHO AT THE CASTLE?

Skilled Craftspeople made many things inside the castle: cloth, metal, tools, armor, furniture, leatherwork, etc.

Helpers assisted craftsmen at their work. Many helpers were children.

BLACKSMITH

ORCHARD

STABLES

KENNELS

LEATHER WORKER

CLOTH DYER

CARPENTER

FALCONER

PEOPLE HAVE ALMOST EVERYTHING THEY NEED INSIDE THE CASTLE WALL.

EXCEPT CLOTHES LIKE THAT!

FISH POND

WHAT WERE CASTLES FOR?

A castle was the center of life for a whole community. Sometimes, but not always, a town grew up around a castle.

WE WORK FOR THE CASTLE.

WE EAT AND SLEEP HERE, TOO.

Suddenly, trumpets blared.
The lord of the castle was riding out of the gate
with his army thundering behind him.
Everyone stopped working to wave and cheer.
Tom said that Lord Robert and his men
were going to help fight a war for the king.

THE LORD FIGHTS FOR THE KING.

AND WE KNIGHTS FIGHT FOR THE LORD.

SPEAKING OF KNIGHTS, I HAVE HUNDREDS OF THEM IN MY SHOP.

YOU MUST BE A VERY POWERFUL LORD!

Fighters

Lord Robert
owns the castle and its lands

Knights
sworn to fight for Lord Robert

Men at Arms
Foot soldiers employed by Lord Robert

Squires
Knights' helpers

Peg explained that while the lord was away,
Lady Anne was in charge of the castle.
I knew Arnold wanted to help her,
so I led everyone up to the tower
where the lady was looking out over the land.

THIS IS **SO** EXCITING! THANKS FOR BRINGING US ON THIS ADVENTURE, ARNOLD!

NO PROBLEM, CRYSTAL. ADVENTURE IS ARNOLD'S MIDDLE NAME!

NO, IT ISN'T. IT'S MATTHEW.

W HO'S WHO AT THE CASTLE?

Lady Anne
Wife of Lord Robert. She supervises the servants and makes sure everything inside the castle runs smoothly.
   When her husband is away, she is responsible for the protection of the castle, too.

Constable Peter
commander of the garrison

The Garrison
the guards and soldiers who are always there to defend the castle

From the castle top, we could see for miles. Suddenly, hoofbeats sounded in the distance. A soldier yelled, "It's Baron Griffin and his army! He is going to try to capture the castle!"

BARON GRIFFIN AND LORD ROBERT HAVE BEEN ENEMIES FOR A LONG TIME.

EACH ONE WANTS THE OTHER'S LAND AND CASTLE...

NOW THE BARON HAS FINALLY MADE HIS MOVE!

WHO'S <u>NOT</u> IN THE CASTLE?

Baron Griffin

WHAT WERE CASTLES FOR?

A castle was the <u>command post</u> used to <u>control</u> the lord's land.

FROM THE CASTLE WE CAN SEE...

IF WORKERS IN THE FIELDS ARE DOING THEIR JOBS...

IF POACHERS ARE HUNTING IN LORD ROBERT'S FORESTS...

IF ANYONE COMES ONTO LORD ROBERT'S ESTATE.

FROM THE CASTLE WE CAN SEND OUT SOLDIERS TO HANDLE PROBLEMS.

We looked out over the fields.
Peasants were hurrying away from
the approaching army.
As they ran, they loaded crops into carts
and drove cows and sheep toward the castle.

Just as the last peasants ran inside the wall, the baron's army arrived. The order went out: "Close the gate!" The drawbridge was pulled up. The portcullis came down with a bang. We were under siege!

Lady Anne went to her private chamber and called in the constable and her adviser, Sir Gilbert. I always give good advice, so I went along to help plan the strategy to defend the castle.
Quickly, Lady Anne wrote a letter to Lord Robert.

THE SOLDIERS MUST SHOOT ARROWS FROM THE TOP OF THE CASTLE, MY LADY.

QUITE RIGHT, STRANGE KNIGHT.

CONSTABLE PETER, GIVE THE ORDER!

AT ONCE, MY LADY.

WHO'S WHO IN THE CASTLE?

SIR GILBERT
Lord Robert's uncle who lives in the castle

LADIES-IN-WAITING
companions and helpers to Lady Anne

The army was using the towers to get into our castle.
From behind the battlements of the castle,
our small garrison could fight off a huge army.
But if the army got inside, the castle guards
would be outnumbered.
They wouldn't have a chance in hand-to-hand combat.
I, Ms. Frizzle, knew one thing for sure —
we *had* to keep the baron's troops *out*!

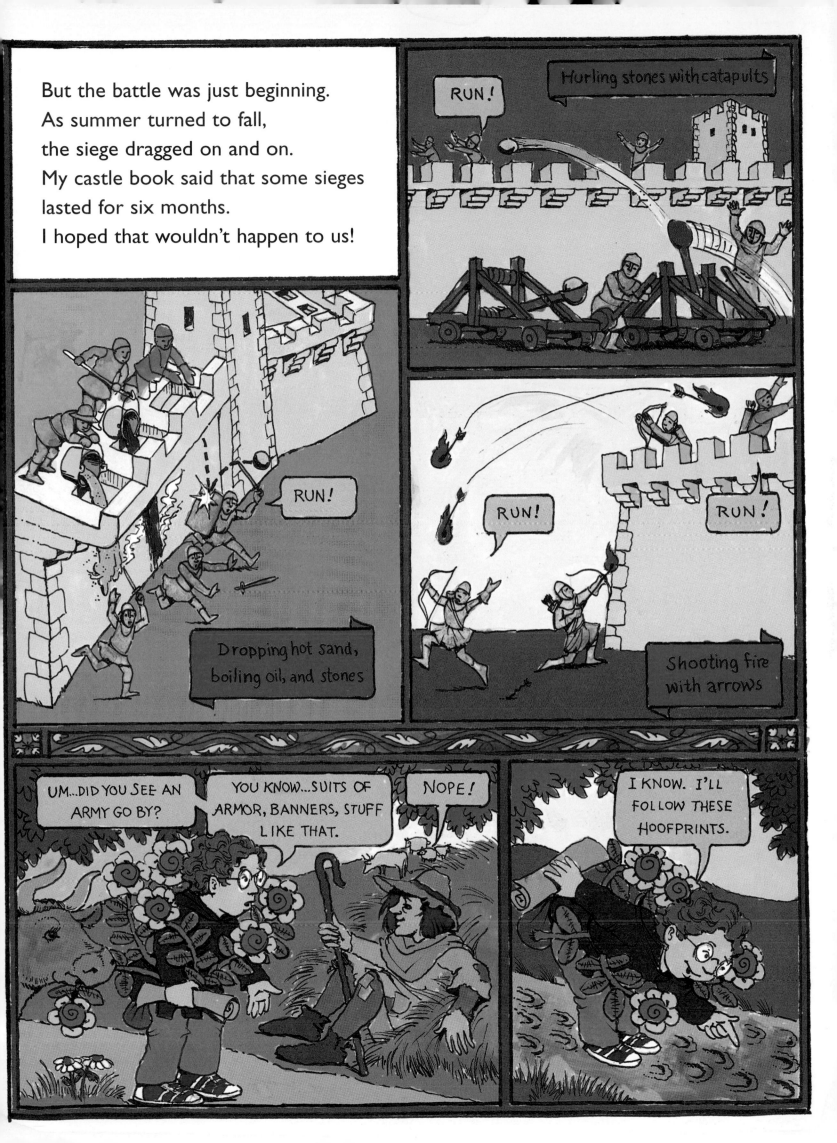

But the battle was just beginning.
As summer turned to fall,
the siege dragged on and on.
My castle book said that some sieges
lasted for six months.
I hoped that wouldn't happen to us!

RUN!

Hurling stones with catapults

RUN!

Dropping hot sand, boiling oil, and stones

RUN!

RUN!

Shooting fire with arrows

UM...DID YOU SEE AN ARMY GO BY?

YOU KNOW...SUITS OF ARMOR, BANNERS, STUFF LIKE THAT.

NOPE!

I KNOW. I'LL FOLLOW THESE HOOFPRINTS.

Luckily, we had plenty of water.
It came from a well under the castle.
Our food was running low.
The besieging army was hungry, too.
But the baron would not give up.
The siege wasn't over yet!

DESIGNED FOR DEFENSE

EARLY DESIGN:
WATER COMES FROM OUTSIDE

PROBLEM:
Attackers can dam up the water or even poison it.

RESULT:
Outsiders can't get to the water.

LATER DESIGN:
WATER SOURCE INSIDE WALLS

Now Baron Griffin gave a new order.
He told his soldiers to a dig a tunnel
right up to the castle.
Since the Baron's men were underground,
our lookouts couldn't see them.

The enemy soldiers began digging a hole under the castle.
As the men enlarged the space, they used wooden posts to prop up the heavy stone.

When the space was large enough, the diggers made a fire to burn up the posts.

The posts crumbled into ashes, and the stone wall fell down.

Just then we heard the blare of bugles. The king's war was over, and Arnold had delivered Lady Anne's letter! Lord Robert had arrived with his army!

Lord Robert called for a celebration.
There was hardly any food left in the castle,
but the army had brought back new supplies.
The castle people feasted with gusto —
they'd been hungry for such a long time.

THE GREAT HALL
Lords, ladies, clergy, and guests feasted here.

THE HIGH TABLE

Hollowed-out slabs of bread served as plates.

CENTER TABLE

WHAT THEY ATE
1. Roast Swan and...
2. Pheasant presented with feathers on
3. Rich stews of meat, vegetables, and spices served on bread
4. Grilled fish
5. Dried fruits and nuts
6. Pigeons baked in fancy pastry
7. Wine, ale — only rich people had glasses. Others drank from leather tankards or wooden goblets.

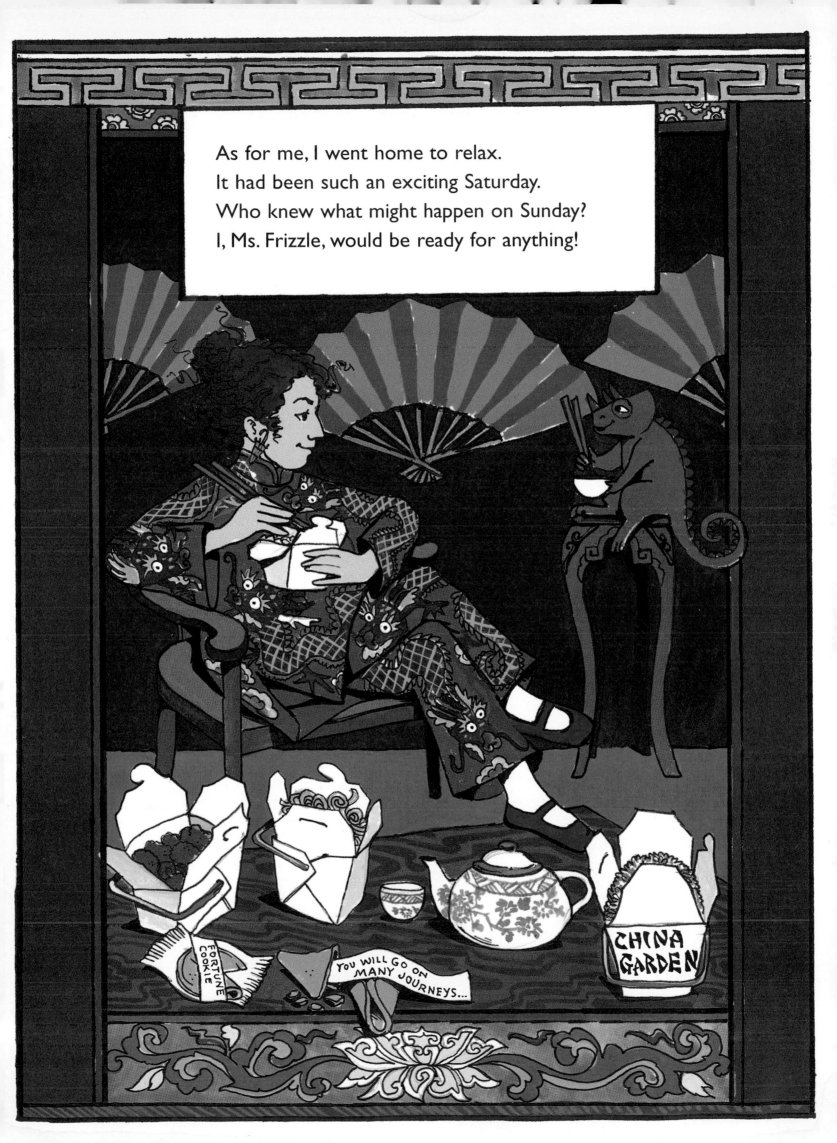

As for me, I went home to relax.
It had been such an exciting Saturday.
Who knew what might happen on Sunday?
I, Ms. Frizzle, would be ready for anything!

DON'T BELIEVE EVERYTHING YOU READ!

(Especially in this book)

Some things are just pretend, and others need a little explanation.

♥ At least one thing in this book is just pretend. A wristwatch cannot take you back in time — no matter how fancy it is. (Not even if it tells the date, reads your e-mail, and knows how old your sister is.)

♥ In this book, it may seem as if the people besieging the castle are bad and the ones inside the castle are good. However, they are all probably just about the same. For all we know, Lord Robert might attack Baron Griffin's castle some day.

♥ The people in this book all talk to each other easily. But in medieval England, people spoke an old kind of English. It would have been hard for Ms. Frizzle's group and the castle dwellers to understand each other.

♥ You might not have liked life in a castle. It was cold, smelly, and uncomfortable. People did not take baths very often, and they usually had fleas. Only the nobles had beds; others slept on the floor. Also, there was no TV in those days.

♥ One thing is true that may seem false. People sometimes think that women had no power in the olden days. But the lady of the castle really was the boss when the lord went away.

♥ It is also true that Arnold was brave. We're so proud of him.

♥ And Ms. Frizzle really did wear a knight's armor. You know how she loves dressing up!

MS. FRIZZLE'S ADVENTURES MEDIEVAL CASTLE

JOANNA·SCRIPTIT BRUCE·PINXIT